# *Best Inspirational Life Quotes*

## Volume 1

• • • • •

## By Sunny

To order additional copies of this book, contact:
Xlibris
AU TFN: 1 800 844 927 (Toll Free inside Australia)
AU Local: 02 8310 8187 (+61 2 8310 8187 from outside Australia)
www.xlibris.com.au
Orders@Xlibris.com.au

ISBN:   Softcover      979-8-3694-9594-0
        Hardcover     979-8-3694-9626-8
        EBook         979-8-3694-9595-7

Library of Congress Control Number: 2024907059

Print information available on the last page

Rev. date:  04/23/2024

To my beloved granddaughters.

**Isabelle, Felicity, and Mia**

ALWAYS DO GOOD WHEREVER YOU GO.

ALWAYS SEE BEAUTY IN EVERYTHING
YOU SEE AND EVERYONE YOU MEET.

BE QUICK TO FORGIVE AND FORGET.

HAPPINESS AND INNER PEACE
WILL BE YOUR REWARD.

WE EAT TO LIVE, WE DON'T LIVE TO EAT, SO MAKE SURE YOU EAT HEALTHY, TO STAY HEALTHY, TO REGENERATE AND NOT DEGENERATE, SO

THINK HEALTHY.

ONE APPLE A DAY

KEEPS THE DOCTOR AWAY.

FIVE APPLES A DAY

THE DOCTOR WILL BE ON HIS WAY.

FASTING FROM TOXIC FOODS DETOXIFIES YOU.
FASTING FROM NEGATIVE THOUGHTS PURIFIES YOU.

COMPLIMENTS UPLIFT. CRITICISMS DEFLATE.
BE AN UPLIFTER NOT A DEFLATOR.

WORDS ARE POWERFUL.

CHOOSE THE RIGHT ONES.

TO BE CONTENT WITH VERY LITTLE IS
THE TRUE SECRET OF HAPPINESS.

THE SKY IS NEVER TOO DARK FOR TOO LONG.

AFTER THE RAIN, COMES THE SUN.

LOOK ALWAYS AT THE BRIGHT SIDE.

THERE IS ALWAYS LIGHT AT THE
END OF THE TUNNEL.

DON'T SETTLE FOR LESS THAN THE BEST.

YOU OWE IT TO YOURSELF.

AIM FOR THE STARS, AND DON'T COMPROMISE.

IF YOU FAIL, KEEP TRYING UNTIL YOU SUCCEED.

SELF DETERMINATION IS A GREAT ATTRIBUTE.

NEVER GIVE UP TRYING.

HE WHO NEVER MADE A MISTAKE,
NEVER MADE A DISCOVERY.

WHATEVER YOU PERCEIVE YOU RECEIVE. BEWARE

IF YOU CANNOT LOVE YOURSELF, HOW
CAN YOU LOVE ANOTHER?

WE ALL MIRROR EACH OTHER.

WHAT YOU SEE IN OTHERS IS WHAT YOU ARE.

BE A LEADER, NOT A FOLLOWER.

STAND YOUR GROUND AND BE DIFFERENT.

VIVE LA DIFFÉRENCE!

POLITICS PLUS RELIGION, EQUAL WARS AND MISERY.

NO ONE IS A WINNER, EVERY ONE IS A LOSER.

THE SOONER WE LEARN, THE BETTER WE THRIVE.

YOU WANT PEACE IN THIS WORLD.

ELIMINATE POLITICS AND RELIGION.

THEY ARE THE TWO WORST EVILS IN THIS WORLD.

BE KIND, BE GENEROUS, BE LOVING. THEY ARE YOUR BEST ATTRIBUTES IN LIFE.

EVERYONE IS YOUR TEACHER.

BLESS THE PEOPLE WHO GIVE
YOU A HARD TIME IN LIFE.

THEY ARE THE PEOPLE WHO HELP
SHAPE YOUR FUTURE.

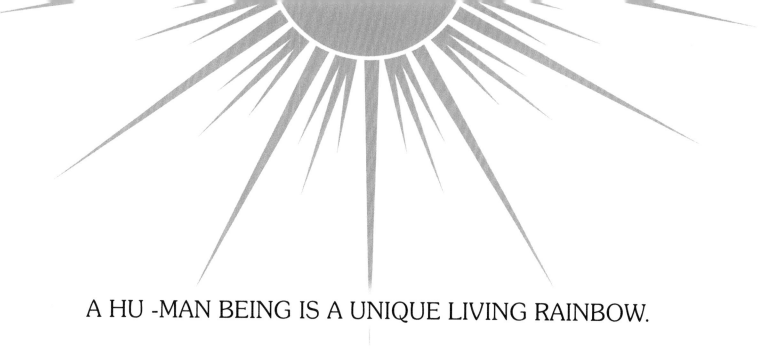

A HU -MAN BEING IS A UNIQUE LIVING RAINBOW.

EACH OF THE SEVEN CHAKRAS HAS
ITS OWN INDIVIDUAL COLOUR.

CAN YOU SEE HOW BEAUTIFUL YOU ARE!

KEEP SHINING.

FRIENDSHIP IS SACRED. HONOUR IT.

TO SLEEP IN A COMFORTABLE BED
AT NIGHT IS A BLESSING.

TO HAVE A GLASS OF WATER NEXT
TO YOU IS A BLESSING.

TO HAVE INNER PEACE IS EVEN
A GREATER BLESSING.

CONSIDER YOURSELF EXTREMELY LUCKY,
AND VERY BLESSED INDEED.

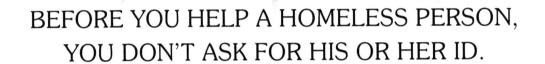

BEFORE YOU HELP A HOMELESS PERSON,
YOU DON'T ASK FOR HIS OR HER ID.

WHETHER HE OR SHE IS

A CHRISTIAN, A JEW, A MUSLIM, A HINDU OR AN
ATHEIST, YOU STILL ATTEND TO HIS OR HER NEEDS.,

THIS IS THE POWER OF HUMANITY.

WE ARE ALL HERE TO SERVE.

WHEN GOD CLOSES A DOOR, HE
OPENS ANOTHER ONE.

TRUST, ALL IS WELL.

MY FATHER IN HEAVEN IS THE RICHEST FATHER IN THE UNIVERSE. HE ATTENDS TO ALL MY NEEDS. HE HAS NEVER LET ME DOWN.

RELIGION DIVIDES. SPIRITUALITY UNITES.

LIFE IS LIKE A BOOMERANG. WHAT YOU THROW OUT THERE ALWAYS COMES BACK TO YOU.

TO BE EXTREMELY GENEROUS IS NOT TO BE
GENEROUS TO A FAULT. IT IS A GREAT VIRTUE.

A FRUIT TREE GIVES AN ABUNDANCE OF FRUITS.

MOTHER NATURE IS EXTREMELY GENEROUS.

EMULATE HER EXAMPLE.

KEEP GIVING, AND NEVER STOP GIVING.

THE MORE YOU GIVE, THE MORE YOU GET.

THIS IS THE LAW OF ATTRACTION.

AGE IS JUST A NUMBER.

YOUR ATTITUDE IS WHAT DEFINES
YOU AS YOUNG OR OLD.

ALWAYS FIND SOMETHING TO LAUGH ABOUT.

LAUGHTER IS A GREAT HEALER.

BE AS CRYSTAL CLEAR IN ALL YOUR DEALINGS.

SUCCESS IS YOUR REWARD.

A POOR MAN CAN SEE THE SUNRISE AND
THE SUNSET FROM HIS SHACK.

A KING CAN ONLY SEE EITHER FROM HIS ROOM.

YOUR INTUITION IS YOUR MOST
POWERFUL INSTRUCTOR

ALWAYS BE AWARE OF THIS PRECIOUS INNER VOICE.

BE MINDFUL OF WHAT YOU SAY.

WORDS ARE VERY POWERFUL.

DO NOT ATTRACT ANY UNDESIRABLE
EXPERIENCES TO YOURSELF, ESPECIALLY WHEN
UTTERING THE WORD "I AM". BEWARE.

NEVER LEAVE FOR TOMORROW WHAT YOU
CAN DO TODAY. TIME IS OF VALUE.

DO NOT FEEL BAD IF YOU EXPRESS AN OPINION
THAT YOU WOULD NEVER NORMALLY DO.

SOMEONE PRESENT NEEDED TO HEAR IT.

YOU WERE USED TO RELAY THE
MESSAGE BY THE UNIVERSE.

LIFE IS LIKE A GAME OF PASS THE PARCEL.

WE ARE ALL LINKED TO ONE ANOTHER.

IT IS WHAT YOU COULD CALL A CHAIN REACTION.

SOMETIMES YOU OVERHEAR SOMEONE TALKING.

IT IS NOT A COINCIDENCE.

THERE LIES A MESSAGE FOR YOU.

TAKE HEED OF IT.

DO NOT DISMISS IT.

"EMPATHY IS FAR BETTER THAN SYMPATHY.

IT PLACES YOU IN SOMEONE ELSE'S SHOES.

IT CREATES BETTER UNDERSTANDING."

WE NEED MORE OF IT IN THIS WORLD.

PROBLEMS ARE BLESSINGS IN DISGUISE. THEY MAKE YOU STRONGER NOT WEAKER. YOU ONLY REALISE THAT WHEN YOU LOOK BACK AFTER FEW DAYS, FEW WEEKS, FEW MONTHS, OR EVEN FEW YEARS LATER ON DOWN THE LINE. BE GRATEFUL AND BLESS EVERY ONE OF THEM.

NEVER DESPAIR.

"MEDITATE BEFORE YOU MEDICATE"

WORDS ARE POWERFUL, CHOOSE THE RIGHT ONES

WITH LOVE IN YOUR HEART YOU CAN CONQUER

THE WORLD.

BE FEARLESS.

DO NOT ALLOW FEAR TO CONTROL YOUR ACTIONS.

YOU HAVE WITHIN YOU A SUPER POWER
THAT CAN MOVE MOUNTAINS FOR YOU.

BELIEVE AND YOU CAN ACHIEVE.

YOU ARE RESPONSIBLE FOR YOUR OWN ACTIONS.

NO ONE ELSE IS.

YOU REAP WHAT YOU SOW.

YOUR THOUGHTS ARE VERY POWERFUL.

YOU ATTRACT YOUR VERY OWN EXPERIENCE.

BE A WINNER, NOT A WINGER.

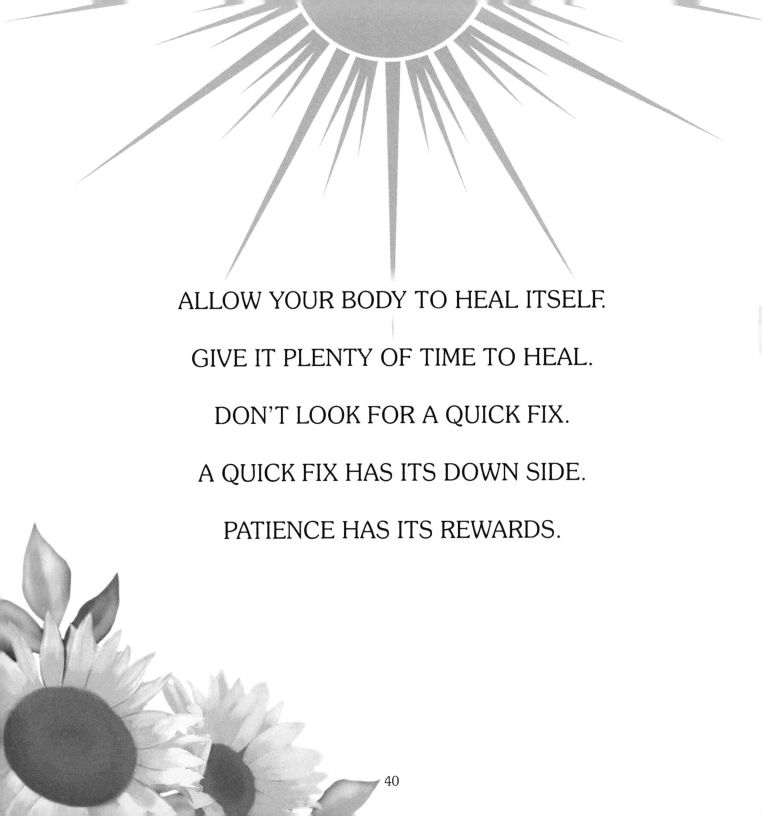

ALLOW YOUR BODY TO HEAL ITSELF.

GIVE IT PLENTY OF TIME TO HEAL.

DON'T LOOK FOR A QUICK FIX.

A QUICK FIX HAS ITS DOWN SIDE.

PATIENCE HAS ITS REWARDS.

A HAPPY ATTITUDE IS THE ONLY ATTITUDE.

EXPECT MIRACLES.

GOD IS AWARE OF ALL YOUR NEEDS.

LET HIM LEAD THE WAY.

LIFE IS LIKE A PIÑATA, FULL OF SURPRISES.

LET IT SURPRISE YOU.

KEEP YOUR WORRIES TO YOURSELF.

NO ONE IS INTERESTED TO HEAR THEM.

SOON YOU WILL FORGET THEM.

YOU DON'T NEED SOMEONE TO REMIND YOU.

LAUGHTER IS THE BEST MEDICINE.

DO NOT TAKE LIFE TOO SERIOUSLY ALL THE TIME.

ALLOW SOME FUN INTO YOUR LIFE.

EVERYONE OF US HAS HIS OWN JOURNEY IN LIFE.

DO NOT LET SOMEONE ELSE'S JOURNEY
IMPINGE ON YOURS IN LIFE.

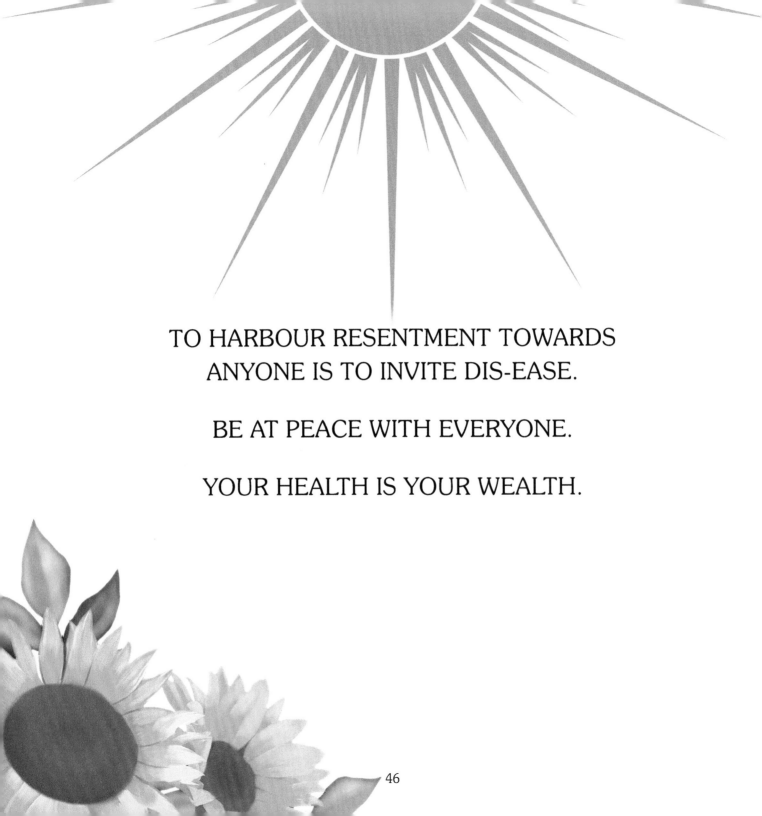

TO HARBOUR RESENTMENT TOWARDS
ANYONE IS TO INVITE DIS-EASE.

BE AT PEACE WITH EVERYONE.

YOUR HEALTH IS YOUR WEALTH.

GOD IS LOVE, AND HIS LOVE IS UNCONDITIONAL

EVERY DAY IS A GOOD DAY TO SERVE.

DO IT WITH LOVE.

WHEN READING THE WORD "IMPOSSIBLE",
MAKE SURE YOU ALWAYS READ IT THIS WAY "I M
POSSIBLE, BECAUSE THIS IS THE ONLY WAY".

PRAYING IS CALLING GOD ON THE PHONE, AND
LEAVING A MESSAGE ON HIS ANSWERING MACHINE.

INTUITION IS GOD CALLING YOU BACK
WITH THE ANSWER – HAVE FAITH

TO ALL MY READERS,

WITH ALL MY LOVE, MAY GOD ALWAYS BLESS
YOU, AND PROTECT YOU. HAVE FAITH.

ALL IS WELL


SUNNY

Printed and bound by CPI Group (UK) Ltd, Croydon, CR0 4YY

30/04/2025

01857727-0001